I0555410

COOKING
MADE EASY WITH THE USE OF
CANISTERS

COOKING
MADE EASY WITH THE USE OF
CANISTERS

TRESSIE L. SANDERS

ARPress
ILLUMINATING IDEAS,
EMPOWERING VOICES

Copyright © 2024 by Tressie L. Sanders

All rights reserved. No part of this publication may be reproduced, distributed, or transmitted in any form or by any means, including photocopying, recording, or other electronic or mechanical methods, without the prior written permission of the copyright owner or the publisher, except in the case of brief quotations embodied in critical reviews and certain other noncommercial uses permitted by copyright law. For permission requests, write to the publisher, addressed "Attention: Permissions Coordinator," at the address below.

ARPress
45 Dan Road Suite 5
Canton MA 02021

Hotline: 1(888) 821-0229
Fax: 1(508) 545-7580

Ordering Information:

Quantity sales. Special discounts are available on quantity purchases by corporations, associations, and others. For details, contact the publisher at the address above.

Printed in the United States of America.

ISBN-13:   Softcover   979-8-89356-907-0
            eBook   979-8-89356-908-7

Library of Congress Control Number: 2024904918

In my cookbook, I will teach you how to cook some of your favorite foods, such as chicken, catfish, pork chops, onion rings, steak, tilapia, etc., easier with the use of canisters.

Table of Contents

PREFACE

In my cookbook, I show you how to make cooking easier. Everybody has certain foods they love to eat. Some of the foods I love to eat are chicken, pork chops, steak, catfish, tilapia, salmon, roast, and hush puppies.

I created catfish coating, chicken coating, dried basil, restaurant black pepper, creole seasoning, and onion powder mixture. All of the ingredients are given for catfish coating, chicken coating, and dried basils, restaurant black pepper, creole seasoning, and onion powder mixture.

Canisters are used to hold your catfish coating chicken coating, dried basil, restaurant black pepper, creole seasoning, and onion powder mixture. You can make as much as you want. You can also use canisters for corn meals, all-purpose flour, granulated sugar, etc.

One of the first things you should do is buy canisters. I use more than one size canister. For the foods I cook often, I use a large canister. For example, if I fry chicken often, I don't want to keep making the coating every time I fry chicken. If you noticed, I give you a lot of goods you can cook with chicken coating you need to cook the amount of food you want to cook. I always leave a small amount of water in the container used to wash my chicken to keep the chicken moist because the coating will cling better if the chicken is moist.

Under "Catfish Coating," I give you the ingredients and the amount to use if you want to cook a few pieces of catfish or a lot of catfish. Under "Ingredients x 4," I multiplied Ingredients x 1 by 4. Under Ingredients x 8, I multiplied Ingredients x 1 by 8. You can make as much catfish coating as you like, but make sure none of the ingredients have expired. If baking powder expires on October 10, 2016, Lawry's Seasoned Salt expires on November 10, 2016, restaurant black pepper expires on September 10, 2016, and corn meal expires on January 10, 2017, you will place the expiration date September 10, 2016, on your canisters as the date that your catfish coating will expire because it has the earliest expiration date. Try to buy ingredients that have long expiration dates. Do the same for chicken coating, dried basil, restaurant black pepper, creole seasoning, and onion powder mixture.

In my book, I will give you some of the uses for catfish coating, chicken coating, and dried basil, restaurant black pepper, creole seasoning, and onion powder mixture.

When cooking broiled Parmesan chicken, broiled Parmesan catfish fillets, and broiled Parmesan tilapia fillets, first find the recipe you are going to make. For example, if you are going to make broiled Parmesan chicken, look for my recipe for broiled Parmesan chicken. This mixture is a mixture you have already made. It is in one of your canisters. All you have to do is to take 1 teaspoons of the mixture you have already made instead of adding them individually because you have already combined them in your canister. You do the same when cooking broiled Parmesan catfish fillets and broiled Parmesan tilapia fillets.

CATFISH COATING

Ingredients x 1

- 1 tablespoon & 1 ½ teaspoon baking powder
- 1 ¼ teaspoons Lawry's Seasoned Salt
- 1 tablespoon & 1 teaspoon restaurant black pepper
- 1 ⅜ cups & 1 ½ teaspoons corn meal

Ingredients x 8

- ¾ cup baking powder
- 3 tablespoons & 1 teaspoon Lawry's Seasoned Salt
- ½ cup, 2 tablespoons, & 2 teaspoons restaurant black pepper
- ¼ cups corn meal

Ingredients x 4

- ¼ cup & 2 tablespoons baking powder
- 1 tablespoon & 2 teaspoons Lawry's Seasoned Salt
- ¼ cup, 1 tablespoon, & 1 teaspoon restaurant black pepper
- 5 ½ cups & 2 tablespoons corn meal

Directions:

Mix together corn meal, baking powder, restaurant black pepper, and Lawry's Seasoned Salt.

Canisters used for:

- Catfish coating
- Chicken coating
- Seasoning for boiled Parmesan chicken, broiled Parmesan catfish fillets, broiled Parmesan tilapia fillets
- Corn meal
- All-purpose flour
- Cake flour
- Pure cane or granulated sugar

CHICKEN COATING

Ingredients x 1

- 1 ½ cups Gold Medal Sifted Self-Rising Flour
- 4 teaspoons or 1 tablespoon & 1 teaspoon restaurant black pepper
- ½ teaspoon Lawry's Seasoned Salt

Ingredients x 12

- 18 cups Gold Medal Sifted-Rising Flour
- 1 cup restaurant black pepper
- 2 tablespoons Lawry's Seasoned Salt

Ingredients x 6

- 9 cups Gold Medal Sifted-Rising Flour
- ½ cup restaurant black pepper
- 1 tablespoon Lawry's Seasoned Salt

Directions:

1. Mix together the Gold Medal Sifted-Rising Flour, restaurant black pepper, and Lawry's Seasoned Salt.
2. *Gold Medal Pre-sifted Self-Rising Flour is on the flour bag, but I always sift the flour before making my Chicken Coating.
3. I stir in the other ingredients.

Dried basil, restaurant black pepper, creole seasoning, onion powder mixture used for:

- Broiling Parmesan catfish fillets
- Broiling Parmesan chicken
- Broiling Parmesan tilapia fillets

Chicken coating used for:

- Coating pot roast
- Frying chicken
- Frying chicken tenders
- Frying hush puppies
- Frying onion rings
- Frying pork chops
- Frying steak
- Smothering chicken
- Smothering pork chops
- Smothering steak

Catfish coating used for:

- Baking catfish fillets
- Frying catfish fillets
- Frying hush puppies

CHICKEN ALFREDO

Ingredients

- 2 pounds boneless, skinless chicken breasts
- 4 tablespoons Extra Virgin Olive Oil
- 1 cup Imperial Spread
- 4 cups freshly grated Parmesan cheese
- 2 cups heavy cream
- ⅛ teaspoon salt
- 1 teaspoon restaurant black pepper
- ½ pound fettucine

Directions:

1. Heat oil in a large skillet.
2. Cut chicken breasts into strips. Season strips with salt and pepper.
3. Cook on medium to low heat until done. Do not overcook; no redness inside of chicken strips; light brown on the outside.

Sauce

1. Melt Imperial Spread in saucepan.
2. Add cheese and cream. Cook over low heat, stirring constantly. Do not boil.
3. Add chicken strips to sauce. Cook over low heat until slightly thickened. Set aside.

Fettucine

- Cook fettucine according to package directions.
- When ready to serve, serve sauce over fettucine.

BROILED PARMESAN CHICKEN, BROILED PARMESAN CATFISH FILLETS, BROILED PARMESAN TILAPIA FILLETS

Ingredients x 1

- ½ teaspoon dried basil
- ½ teaspoon restaurant black pepper
- ¼ creole seasoning
- ¼ teaspoon onion powder

IIngredients x 20

- 3 tablespoons and 1 teaspoon dried basil
- 3 tablespoons and 1 teaspoon restaurant black pepper
- 1 tablespoon and 2 teaspoons creole seasoning
- 1 tablespoon and 2 teaspoons onion powder

BAKED CHICKEN QUARTERS

Ingredients

- 1/3 cup lemon juice (I use 2 lemons)
- 1/3 cup Extra Virgin Olive Oil
- 1 ½ teaspoons dried leaf thyme
- 1 ½ teaspoons dried leaf parsley
- 1 teaspoon Lawry's Seasoned Salt
- 8 cloves garlic, grated
- 1 chicken, about 3 ½ to 4 ½ pounds, quartered 1 teaspoon restaurant black pepper

Directions:

1. Heat oven to 375 °F.
2. Combine lemon juice, olive oil, thyme, parsley, Lawry's Seasoned Salt, black pepper, and garlic.
3. Toss the chicken with the mixture; arrange in a baking dish.
4. Bake for about 1 ½ hours to 2 hours, turning approximately halfway through cooking. The chicken will be tender when done.

CHICKEN STEW

Ingredients

- 1 whole chicken (cut up) or chicken parts
- 1 teaspoon salt (plain)
- 2 teaspoons restaurant black pepper
- 3 tablespoons Extra Virgin Olive Oil (cooking chicken)
- 1 medium onion (broken in a small pieces)
- 3 tablespoons Extra Virgin Olive Oil (browning flour)
- 4 tablespoons all-purpose flour
- 1 red bell pepper (chopped)
- 1 yellow pepper (chopped)
- 1 green pepper (chopped)
- ½ small carrot (chopped)
- ½ stalk celery (chopped)
- 2 teaspoons seasoned pepper
- 1 teaspoons creole seasoning
- 1 ½ cups water

Directions:

1. Season chicken with plain salt and restaurant black pepper. Place 2 tablespoons Extra Virgin Olive Oil in skillet; heat until hot. Place seasoned chicken in Extra Virgin Olive Oil. Lightly brown chicken on all sides.
2. Place onion in skillet with chicken; cook until lucent.
3. Pour 3 tablespoons of Extra Virgin Olive Oil in separate small skillet; add 4 tablespoons of flour to Extra Virgin Olive Oil. Cook until lightly browned.
4. Add gravy to chicken and onion in large skillet; stir. Add vegetables, seasoned pepper, creole seasoning, and water to large skillet; bring to a boil on high heat.
5. Reduce heat to medium; cook for 30 minutes. Reduce heat to low; cook for 30 minutes or until tender. Stir occasionally.

CHICKEN TENDERS

Ingredients

- 2 cups chicken coating
- Boneless, skinless chicken breasts (cut in strips) 3 ½ to 4 pounds
- Buttermilk for soaking chicken (approximately 2 cups)
- Buttermilk for drizzling chicken coating (can use buttermilk used for soaking chicken)
- Canola Oil (I use 6 to 7 cups)

Directions:

1. Put 2 cups of chicken in a bowl. (When using my chicken coating, you can cook as many chickens as you want, add as much chicken coating as you are using.)
2. Soak chicken tenders in buttermilk for 20 to 25 minutes. Dizzle a few drops of buttermilk onto chicken coating in bowl.
3. Fluff the buttermilk drops into chicken coating with a fork until little crumbles form.
4. Dip each piece of chicken into chicken coating fluffed with buttermilk drops.
5. Preheat oil in work until temperature reaches 350 °F. Deep fry tenders until golden brown, approximately 6 to 8 minutes.
6. Remove tenders from wok and cool on paper towel.

BAKED CHICKEN WINGS

Ingredients

- 6 tablespoons Extra Virgin Olive Oil
- 1 tablespoon onion powder
- 2 teaspoons Lawry's Seasoned Salt
- 1 teaspoon garlic powder
- 1 tablespoon restaurant black pepper
- 21 to 24 wings

Directions:

1. Preheat oven to 425 °F.
2. Combine olive oil, onion powder, seasoned salt, garlic powder, and black pepper in large bowl. Add chicken wings to olive oil mixture; stir until chicken wings are well-coated.
3. Bake chicken wings, uncovered, in 15 ¼ x 10 ½ x 2 inches stainless steel baking dish in preheated oven for 1 ½ hours or until tender.

BROILED PARMESAN CATFISH FILLETS

Ingredients

- Extra Virgin Olive Oil Spray
- 1 cup freshly grated Parmesan cheese
- 4 tablespoon Imperial Spread, softened
- ¼ cup light mayonnaise
- 2 tablespoon fresh lemon juice (approx. 1 lemon)
- ½ teaspoon dried basil
- 1 ½ teaspoon restaurant black pepper (1 ½ teaspoons of mixture)
- ¼ teaspoon creole seasoning
- ¼ teaspoon onion powder
- 2 pounds boneless, skinless catfish fillets

Directions:

1. Preheat oven's broiler (Hi setting). Spray Extra Virgin Olive Oil Spray on bottom and top of broiling pan.
2. In a small bowl, mix together Parmesan cheese, Imperial Spread, mayonnaise, lemon juice, dried basil, black pepper, creole seasoning, and onion powder.
3. Arrange fillets in a single layer on prepared broiler pan. Spread approximately one half of Parmesan mixture on top of catfish fillets. Place catfish fillets over; spread remaining Parmesan mixture over catfish fillets. Broil for 5 to 6 more minutes or until topping is golden brown and fish flakes easily with a fork. After broiling is completed, I place catfish fillets in a 13 x 9 x 2 inches glass casserole dish, then I add drippings from bottom tray of broiling pan to casserole dish with catfish fillets.

BROILED PARMESAN CHICKEN

Ingredients

- Extra Virgin Olive Oil Spray
- 1 cup freshly grated Parmesan cheese
- 4 tablespoons Imperial Spread, softened
- ¼ cup light mayonnaise
- 2 tablespoons fresh lemon juice (approx. 1 lemon)
- ½ teaspoon dried basil
- ½ teaspoon restaurant black pepper, 1 ½ teaspoons of mixture
- ¼ teaspoon creole seasoning
- ¼ teaspoon onion powder
- 2 pounds boneless, skinless chicken breasts

Directions:

1. Preheat oven's broiler (Hi setting). Spray Extra Virgin Olive Oil Spray on bottom and top of broiling pan.
2. In a small bowl, mix together Parmesan cheese, Imperial Spread, mayonnaise, lemon juice, dried basil, black pepper, creole seasoning, and onion powder.
3. Arrange chicken breasts in a single layer on prepared broiler pan. Spread approximately one half of Parmesan mixture on top of chicken. Place chicken breasts in oven and broil 6 to 7 minutes. Remove from oven. Turn chicken over; spread remaining Parmesan mixture over chicken. Broil for 4 to 5 minutes or until the topping is golden brown and juices run clear. After broiling is completed, I place chicken breasts in a 13 x 9 x 2 glass casserole dish; then I add drippings from bottom tray of boiling pan to casserole dish with chicken breasts.

BROILED PARMESAN TILAPIA FILLETS

Ingredients

- Extra Virgin Olive Oil Spray
- 1 cup freshly finely shredded Parmesan cheese
- 4 tablespoons Imperial Spread, softened
- ¼ cup light mayonnaise
- 2 tablespoons fresh lemon juice (approx. 1 lemon)
- ½ teaspoon restaurant dried basil
- ½ teaspoon restaurant black pepper (1 ½ teaspoons of mixture)
- ¼ teaspoon creole seasoning
- ¼ teaspoon onion powder
- 2 pounds tilapia boneless fillets

Directions:

1. Preheat oven's broiler (Hi setting). Spray Extra Virgin Olive Oil Spray on bottom and top of broiling pan.
2. In a small bowl, mix together Parmesan cheese, Imperial Spread, mayonnaise, lemon juice, dried basil, black pepper, creole seasoning, and onion powder.
3. Arrange fillets in a single layer on prepared broiler pan. Spread approximately one half of Parmesan mixture on top pf tilapia fillets. Place tilapia fillets in oven and broil 4 to 6 minutes. Remove from oven. Turn fillets over; spread remaining Parmesan mixture over fillets. Broil for 3 to 4 more minutes or until topping is golden brown and fish flakes easily with a fork. After broiling is completed, I place tilapia fillets in a 15 ¼ x 10 ½ x 2 inches stainless steel pan; the I add drippings from bottom tray of broiling pan to stainless steel pan with tilapia fillets.

FRIED CHICKEN

Ingredients

- 1 whole chicken cut up or chicken parts
- 1 ½ cups self-rising flour
- 4 teaspoons restaurant black pepper
- ½ teaspoon Lawry's Seasoned Salt
- 6 to 7 cups canola oil

Directions:

1. Mix flour, black pepper, and Lawry's Seasoned Salt in a bowl.
2. Rinse chicken. Leave small amount of water in bowl with chicken to keep chicken moist.
3. (Flour mixture will cling easier to chicken is moist.)
4. Coat chicken on each side with flour mixture. Shake off excess flour mixture.
5. Heat oil in work until a thermometer reaches a temperature of 350 °F when placed in oil without touching bottom of wok. Cook chicken for approximately 10 minutes or until juices run clear. Can use my chicken coating instead of adding flour, black pepper, and salt above.

BROILED SALMON FILLETS

Ingredients

- 6 (6 ounce) salmon fillets
- 4 tablespoons (¼ cup) Imperial Spread, softened
- 4 tablespoons light mayonnaise
- 2 tablespoons fresh lemon juice
- 1 ½ teaspoons white pepper
- ¼ teaspoon creole seasoning

Ingredients

- 6 (6 ounce) salmon fillets
- 4 tablespoons (¼ cup) Imperial Spread, softened
- 4 tablespoons light mayonnaise
- 2 tablespoons fresh lemon juice
- 1 ½ teaspoons white pepper
- ¼ teaspoon creole seasoning

OVEN-BAKED CATFISH FILLETS

Ingredients

- 6 to 7 skinless, boneless catfish fillets
- Catfish coating
- ¾ cup Imperial Spread

Directions:

1. Preheat oven to 475 °F.
2. Coat catfish with catfish coating.
3. Melt Imperial Spread in 15 ¼ x 10 ½ x 2 inches rectangular stainless steel baking dish in oven until hot.
4. Place catfish top side up in hot melted Imperial Spread in baking dish.
5. Bake, uncovered, for 18 minutes with top side up.
6. Bake, uncovered, for 12 minutes at 475 °F with top side down until golden brown.

BAKED PORK CHOPS

Ingredients

- 4 thin cut pork chops
- 1 can Cream of Mushroom Soup (10 ½ ounce)
- 1 soup can of water
- 2 teaspoons onion powder
- ¼ teaspoon garlic powder
- ½ teaspoon restaurant black pepper

Directions:

1. Preheat oven to 400 °F. Place pork chops in a 3-quart glass rectangular baking dish. Combine Cream of Mushroom Soup, water, onion, powder, garlic powder, and black pepper in bowl. Pour mixture over pork chops.
2. Cover baking dish with foil and bake for 2 hours to 2 hours and 15 minutes, or until pork chops are tender.

COOKED CANNED SALMON

Ingredients

- 3 cans pink salmon
- 4 tablespoons all-purpose flour
- 1 teaspoon restaurant black pepper
- 1 medium onion (broken in pieces)
- Canola oil (4 tablespoons)

Directions:

1. Remove bones from salmon.
2. Brown flour in canola oil.
3. Add onion to flour mixture. Marine onion in flour mixture until soft.
4. Add salmon, salmon juice, and black pepper to flour mixture. Bring to a boil. Reduce heat to medium and cook for approximately 5 minutes.

SALMON CAKES

Ingredients

- 1 (14.75 ounce) can salmon
- ¼ cup all-purpose flour
- 2 eggs, beaten
- ¼ cup onion, finely chopped
- 1 teaspoon restaurant black pepper
- Juice from salmon
- 3 tablespoons canola oil

Directions:

1. Remove bones from salmon. In a mixing bowl, combine flour, eggs, onion, black pepper, salmon, and juice from salmon. Mix thoroughly.

2. Shape into 6 patties. Heat oil in large skillet over medium heat. Fry each patty for 4 minutes on each side or until golden brown.

SMOTHERED CHICKEN AND GRAVY

Ingredients

- 8 pieces of chicken
- 1 medium white onion (broken in pieces)
- Chicken coating (for coating chicken pieces) (3 tablespoons for making gravy)
- ¼ teaspoon Lawry's Seasoned Salt
- 6 to 7 cups canola oil
- 4 garlic cloves (grated)

Directions:

1. Coat chicken pieces with chicken coating. Set it aside.
2. In work, heat canola oil to approximately 350 °F.
3. Add chicken pieces to work. Fry until browned on both sides and juices run clear.
4. Remove chicken pieces; set aside on paper towel. Add 5 tablespoons of oil from wok to large skillet. Add 3 tablespoons of chicken coating and ¼ teaspoon salt to large skillet; stir. Cook chicken coating mixture on medium heat, stirring until golden brown. Add onion pieces and garlic to large skillet. Reduce heat to low; marinate until onion is softened. Add 2 cups of water to large skillet; bring to a boil.
5. Place chicken pieces into large skillet with chicken coating, onion, and garlic mixture. Reduce heat to low. Cover and simmer for 25 to 30 minutes. Turn chicken pieces over after simmering for about 12 minutes. Serve warmly.

BEEF STEW

Ingredients

- Stew meat (2 pounds)
- Seasoning Mix
    - Corn starch (2 teaspoons)
    - Onion powder (1 teaspoon)
    - Garlic powder (½ teaspoon)
    - Paprika (½ teaspoon)
    - Salt (1 teaspoon)
    - Ground sage (¼ teaspoon)
    - Ground cumin (¼ teaspoon)
    - Thyme (¼ teaspoon)
    - Ground coriander (¼ teaspoon)
    - Creole seasoning (1 teaspoon)
    - Restaurant black pepper
        (1 teaspoon)

- Chopped Vegetables
    - Celery (2 stalks)
    - Carrots (3 or 4)
    - Onion (1 large)

- Irish potatoes (4 medium) (cut up; per your preference)
- Jalapeno pepper (1; chopped)
- Extra Virgin Olive Oil (2 tablespoon)
- Water (3 cups)
- Irish potatoes, carrots, celery stalks, onion; should equal to 8 cups

Directions:

1. Brown beef Extra Virgin Olive Oil on medium heat in Dutch oven. Add 3 cups of water and seasoning mix to beef. Bring to a boil. Stir. Cover and simmer for 1 ½ hours.
2. In small skillet, while beef is simmering, add Imperial Spread. Cook Jalapeno pepper in Imperial Spread over low heat until lucent.
3. Add 8 cups (celery, carrots, onion, Irish potatoes) and Jalapeno pepper to Dutch oven. Bring to a boil. Cover and simmer for 1 hour, 20 minutes to 1 hour, 4 minutes. Stir occasionally while stew is simmering. If stew is not thick enough, cook for a few minutes uncovered.

SMOTHERED STEAK AND GRAVY

Ingredients

- 4 rib eye steaks (beaten) (3.5 to 3.6 pounds)
- I medium white onion (broken in pieces)
- Chicken coating (for coating steaks) (3 tablespoons for making gravy)
- ½ teaspoon Lawry's Seasoned Salt
- 6 to 7 cups canola oil
- 4 garlic cloves (grated)

Directions:

1. Beat steaks. Coat steaks with chicken coating. Set it aside.
2. In wok, heat canola oil to approximately 350 °F.
3. Add steaks to the wok. Fry until browned on both sides.
4. Remove steaks; set aside on paper towel. Add 5 tablespoons of oil from wok to large skillet. Add 3 tablespoons of Chicken Coating and ½ teaspoon salt to large skillet; stir. Cook chicken coating mixture on medium heat, stirring until golden brown. Add onion pieces and garlic to large skillet. Reduce heat to low; marinate until onion is softened. Add 3 cups of water to large skillet; bring to a boil.
5. Place steaks into large skillet with chicken coating, onion, and garlic mixture. Reduce heat to low and simmer for 40 to 45 minutes; turn steaks over after simmering for about 18 minutes. Serve warmly.

GROUND BEEF MEAT LOAF

Ingredients

- ¼ cup tomato sauce
- 2 eggs, lightly beaten
- ½ cup almond milk without vanilla
- ½ cup chopped onion
- ½ cup bell pepper, chopped
- 1 ¼ teaspoon salt
- 2 teaspoon restaurant black pepper
- 1 ½ pound ground beef

Directions:

1. In a large bowl, combine tomato sauce, eggs, and almond milk. Stir in onion, bell pepper, salt, and black pepper. Add ground beef. Mix well. Place mixture in an 8x4 inches loaf pan. Lightly pat.
2. Bake in 350 °F oven for 1 hour, 15 minutes to 1 hour, 20 minutes.

Topping

Ingredients

- 1 tablespoon golden brown sugar
- 1 teaspoon dry mustard
- ¼ cup ketchup

Directions:

In a bowl, combine brown sugar, mustard, and ketchup. Spread the meat for 20 minutes before taking the meat loaf out of oven. Let stand a few minutes before serving.

TURKEY MEAT LOAF

Ingredients

- ¼ cup tomato sauce
- 2 eggs, lightly beaten
- ½ cup almond milk without vanilla
- ½ cup chopped onion
- ½ cup bell pepper, chopped
- 1 ¼ teaspoon salt
- 2 teaspoons restaurant black pepper
- 1 ½ pound ground turkey

Directions:

1. In a large bowl, combine tomato sauce, eggs, and almond milk. Stir in onion, bell pepper, salt, and black pepper. Add ground turkey. Mix well. Place mixture in an 8 x 4 inches loaf pan. Lightly pat.
2. Bake in 350 °F oven for 1 hour, 15 minutes to 1 hour, 20 minutes.

Topping

Ingredients

- 1 tablespoon golden brown sugar
- 1 teaspoon dry mustard
- ¼ cup ketchup

Directions:

In a bowl, combine brown sugar, mustard, and ketchup. Spread the meat for 20 minutes before taking the meat loaf out of oven. Let stand a few minutes before serving.

STUFFED BELL PEPPERS

Ingredients

- 4 large bell peppers
- 2 cups cooked rice
- 1 pound ground beef
- ½ cup chopped onion, marinated in 4 tablespoons Imperial Spread
- ½ cup chopped celery, marinated in the above Imperial Spread
- 2 (8 ounce) cans tomato sauce
- 2/3 cup ketchup
- 1 teaspoon salt
- ¼ teaspoon onion powder
- 2 teaspoons restaurant black pepper
- ½ cup water

Directions:

1. Preheat oven to °350 F.
2. Cut thin sliced stem end of each bell pepper to remove top of pepper. Remove seeds and membranes. You may cut thin slice from bottom of peppers so they can stand up straight.
3. Mix cooked rice, raw ground meat, marinated onion and celery, and about 6 tablespoons of tomato sauce. Stuff mixture in the peppers. Put peppers in a deep pan or Pyrex dish. Mix remaining tomato sauce with ketchup, salt, onion powder, black pepper, and ½ cup of water. Pour mixture over stuffed peppers. Cover dish or pan. If there is no cover for dish or pan, cover with foil paper.
4. Bake peppers in pre-heated oven for 1 hour. Peppers should be starting to soften. Remove cover or foil paper. Continue to bake until the meat filling is cooked through, and the peppers are tender (about 20 to 30 minutes). Drizzle spoonful of pan juice over peppers.

FRIED PORK CHOPS
(COOKED IN WOK)

Ingredients

- 8 thinly cut pork chops or (as many as you want)
- (Chicken coating oust enough to coat pork chops)
- Canola oil for frying (I use 6-7 cups)

Directions:

1. Rinse pork chops. Leave a small amount of water in bowl with pork chops to keep pork chops moist. (Flour mixture will cling easier to pork chops if pork chops are moist.)
2. Coat pork chops on each side with chicken coating. Shake off excess chicken coating.
3. Heat canola oil in wok until a thermometer reaches a temperature of 350 °F when placed in oil without touching bottom of wok. Cook pork chops for approximately 10 minutes or until golden brown.

ROASTED TURKEY

Ingredients

- 1 turkey (8 to 10 pounds)
- 6 tablespoons Extra Virgin Olive Oil or ¼ cup plus ⅛ cup
- 1 tablespoon plus 2 teaspoons Lawry's Seasoned Salt
- 1 tablespoon onion powder
- 1 teaspoon garlic powder
- 1 tablespoon restaurant black pepper
- 2 celery stalks, cut up
- 1 large onion, cut in half then cut each half into half

Directions:

1. Preheat oven to 325 °F.
2. Combine olive oil, salt, onion powder, garlic powder, and black pepper in large bowl. Place turkey in large bowl. Rub turkey with olive oil mixture inside and outside until well-coated. Fill turkey with celery and onion.
3. Bake turkey covered in roasting pan for 3 hours. My roasting pan has a cover. My turkey browned in my roasting after cooking 3 hours. If you don't have a roasting pan with a cover, you can cover your turkey with foil paper. Make sure you uncover the turkey 30 minutes before the end of your cooking time to allow your turkey to brown.

GROUND BEEF PASTRIES

Ingredients

- Double my double crust recipe
- 1 pound ground beef
- 4 tablespoons Imperial Spread
- 1/3 cup onion, finely chopped
- ¼ teaspoon salt
- 1 teaspoon restaurant black pepper
- 2 eggs, beaten
- ½ cup Tillamook Sharp Cheddar Cheese (shredded)

Directions:

1. In large skillet, sauté ground beef and onion in Imperial Spread. Stir in salt, black pepper, eggs, cheese, and tomato sauce over medium heat until thoroughly mixed.
2. Roll crust. Cut around pastries using a 4.5 inch round stainless-steel cutter. Place about 2 tablespoons of ground beef mixture on bottom round pastry. Place another round pastry on top. Seal with a fork around the edge of pastry. I dip my fork in a little water to make sealing easier.
3. Bake in 15 ¼ 10 ½ x 2 inch stainless steel baking dish in 375 °F preheated oven for 30 to 35 minutes or until golden brown.

GROUND TURKEY PASTRIES

Ingredients

- Double my double crust recipe
- 1 pound ground turkey
- 4 tablespoons Imperial Spread
- 1/3 cup onion. finely chopped
- ¼ teaspoon salt
- 1 teaspoon restaurant black pepper
- 2 eggs, beaten
- ½ cup Tillamook Sharp Cheddar Cheese (shredded)
- ½ cup tomato sauce

Directions:

1. In large skillet, sauté ground turkey and onion in Imperial Spread. Stir in salt, black pepper, eggs, cheese, and tomato sauce over medium heat until thoroughly mixed.
2. Roll crust. Cut around pastries using a 4.5 inch round stainless-steel cutter. Place about 2 tablespoons of ground turkey mixture on bottom round pastry. Place another round pastry on top. Seal with a fork around the edge of pastry. I dip my fork in a little water to make sealing easier.
3. Bake in a 15 ¼ x 10 ½ x 2 inches stainless steel baking dish in 375 °F preheated oven for 30 to 35 minutes or until golden brown.

MEATBALLS WITH SPAGHETTI SAUCE

Ingredients

- Meatballs
- 1 pound ground beef
- 1 cup chopped onion
- ½ cup almond milk without vanilla
- 1 egg, slightly beaten
- 1 slice of white light bread without rim
- ¼ teaspoon salt
- ¼ teaspoon garlic powder
- ⅛ cup Parmesan cheese
- 3 tablespoons Extra Virgin Olive Oil

Sauce

- 2 (8 ounce) cans tomato sauce
- 3 (14.5 ounce) cans diced tomatoes, undrained
- ⅛ cup Parmesan Cheese, grated
- ½ teaspoon dried basil
- 1 teaspoon dried parsley
- 2 teaspoons restaurant black pepper
- 1 teaspoon salt
- 4 garlic cloves, minced

Directions:

Meatballs

1. In large bowl, mix ground beef, onion, almond milk, egg, light bread, salt, garlic powder, and Parmesan cheese.
2. Shape into 20 to 22 meat balls. Heat oil on medium heat. Cook meatballs on medium heat until browned on each side.

Sauce

1. Stir Parmesan cheese and can of tomato sauce in small microwaveable bowl or glass measuring cup. Microwave for 1 minute to 1 minute, 30 seconds. Then stir until well-blended.
2. Place the other can of tomato sauce, Parmesan cheese mixture, tomatoes (undrained), basil, parsley, black pepper, minced garlic cloves, and salt in Dutch oven. Cover pot and bring to a boil. Add meatballs to sauce. Bring back to a boil. Reduce heat to low; cook covered for 1 hour to 1 hour, 30 minutes. (I like to break up about 4 of the meatballs while in the sauce). Serve sauce and meatballs over warm spaghetti.

TACOS

Ingredients

- 3 tablespoons Extra Virgin Olive Oil
- 1 medium onion (chopped)
- 1 tablespoon McCormick's Seasoned Pepper
- 2 ½ packages McCormick's Taco Seasoning
- 2 cups water
- 5 medium tomatoes, diced
- 2 packages shredded Mexican cheese mix (Kraft)
- 1 package sour cream (1 ounce)
- 1 package pico de gallo (sold by Alberton's)
- 1 package guacamole (sold by Alberton's)
- 1 package 20 soft whole wheat organic taco-size tortillas
- 1 package ground turkey meat (2.5 pounds)
- 2 tablespoons Imperial Spread or Extra Virgin Olive Oil Spray

Directions:

1. Set cheese, sour cream, pico de gallo, tomatoes, and guacamole aside to be used as toppings.
2. In large skillet, heat olive oil. Add chopped onion to skillet. Cook until lucid (see through). Add ground turkey; use spatula to break meat into small pieces (like taco meat). Brown meat and cook through. Once cooked through, add seasoned pepper, taco seasoning, and water to skillet. Stir to mix; bring to a boil. Reduce heat to medium-low; simmer for 5 minutes, stirring occasionally.
3. Warm tortillas in nonstick skillet with Imperial Spread or Extra Virgin Olive Oil Spray or microwave tortillas between two damp pieces of paper towel.

(Occasionally, wipe down skillet between warming shells to prevent burning.)
(Prep tacos. Form taco shells with tortillas. Add meat and toppings and enjoy) Bon Appetit!

(Recipe donated by my daughter)

DEVILED EGGS

Ingredients

- 8 eggs
- 3 tablespoons light mayonnaise
- 3 tablespoons yellow mustard
- 2 tablespoons sweet pickle relish
- 2 teaspoons diced pimientos
- ⅛ teaspoon distilled white vinegar
- Paprika

Directions:

1. Bring eggs to boil in pot; boil eggs for 20 minutes. Cool eggs; peel eggs. Cut eggs lengthwise into 16 halves.
2. Remove yolks from eggs. Combine yolks, mayonnaise, yellow mustard, sweet pickle relish, diced pimientos, and distilled white vinegar.
3. Add yolk mixture to egg white halves with a small scoop. Sprinkle with paprika.

CHICKEN SALAD

Ingredients

- 3 (13 ounce) cans Daily Chef Premium Chunk Chicken Breast
- 2 boiled eggs
- ½ cup light mayonnaise
- 1 teaspoon onion powder
- 1 teaspoon restaurant black pepper
- ¼ cup sweet relish
- 1 tablespoon mustard
- ½ teaspoon distilled white vinegar

Directions:

Combine canned chicken breast, boiled eggs, mayonnaise, onion powder, black pepper, sweet relish, mustard, and distilled vinegar. Refrigerate.

TUNA SALAD

Ingredients

- 5 (5 ounce) cans of Chef Solid White Albacore Tuna
- 2 boiled eggs
- ½ cup light mayonnaise
- 1 teaspoon onion powder
- 1 teaspoon restaurant black pepper
- ¼ cup sweet relish
- 1 tablespoon mustard
- 1 teaspoon distilled white vinegar

Directions:

Combine canned tuna, boiled eggs, mayonnaise, onion powder, black pepper, sweet relish, mustard, and distilled white vinegar. Refrigerate.

CHICKEN FRIED RICE

Ingredients

- 1 egg
- 1 tablespoon canola oil
- 1 sesame oil
- 1 onion, chopped
- 2 cups cooked white rice, cold
- 2 tablespoons soy sauce
- 1 teaspoon restaurant black pepper
- 1 cup cooked, chopped chicken
- ½ cup frozen mixed vegetables, rinsed (I used carrots, corn, and English peas)

Directions:

1. In a small bowl, beat egg. Heat canola oil in a large skillet over medium heat.
2. Add beaten egg and cook until done. Remove egg from skillet; set aside.
3. Heat sesame oil in same skillet; add onion and sauté until soft. Add vegetables to onion; marinate for about 3 minutes. Add rice, soy sauce, black pepper, chicken, and egg (cut up); stir together. Cook over low heat for about 4 to 5 minutes, stirring occasionally.

MACARONI SALAD

Ingredients

- 8 ounces uncooked elbow macaroni
- 2 boiled eggs, cut up in small pieces
- ½ cup light mayonnaise
- 2 tablespoons mustard
- 2 teaspoons restaurant black pepper
- ¼ cup sweet relish
- ½ teaspoon salt
- 1 teaspoon onion powder
- ½ teaspoon garlic powder

Directions:

1. Cook macaroni following elbow macaroni package directions. Drain in colander. Rinse in cold water.
2. Combine all of macaroni salad ingredients.
3. Cover and chill thoroughly.

RICE PILAF

Ingredients

- 2 ½ teaspoons Chicken Flavor Bouillon
- 2 ½ cups boiling water
- 2 tablespoons Imperial Spread
- 1 cup uncooked long grain rice
- 1 teaspoon dried parsley flakes
- ⅛ cup chopped onion
- ⅛ cup chopped celery
- ¼ cup frozen green peas and carrots

Marinate onion and celery until soft in 3 tablespoons Imperial Spread. Add green peas and carrots to onion and celery mixture and cook together for 1 to 2 minutes.

Directions:

1. Mix Chicken Flavor Bouillon and boiling water.
2. Combine Chicken Bouillon mixture and Imperial Spread in saucepan; bring to boil. Stir in rice, parsley flakes, and marinated onion, celery, green peas, and carrots in saucepan; bring back to boil. Cover; reduce heat to low; simmer 20 minutes.

DINNER ROLLS

Ingredients

- 1 packet instant yeast
- 1 cup warm water (105 to 115 °F)
- 2 teaspoons sugar
- ⅛ cup Imperial Spread, softened
- 1 egg
- 1 teaspoon salt
- 3 ½ cups all-purpose flour
- Imperial Spread to grease bowl

Directions:

1. In mixing bowl, dissolve yeast in warm water. Add sugar, Imperial Sperad egg, salt, and flour; beat until smooth.
2. Place dough in bowl that has been greased with Imperial Spread. Turn once to bring greased side up. Cover loosely with foil paper. Refrigerate for 2 hours to allow dough to rise. Remove from refrigerator, punch dough down.
3. Place dough on a clean work surface. Cut dough into 10 portions of dough with bench scraper. Round dough down to 4 to 6 times until dough becomes a round ball. Place balls into 13 x 9 x 2 inch pan. Cover and let rise until doubled in size (1 ½ to 2 hours). Bake rolls in preheated 400 °F oven for 15 to 20 minutes or until golden brown. (I rub Imperial Spread on my rolls when they are done.)

BISCUITS

Ingredients

- 2 cups al-purpose flour
- 1 tablespoon baking powder
- ½ teaspoon salt
- ½ cup Imperial Spread
- ¾ cup buttermilk

Directions:

1. Preheat oven to 450 °F.
2. Sift flour, baking powder, and salt together in large bowl.
3. Cut Imperial Spread into flour mixture with two knives or pastry blender until mixture looks like coarse crumbs.
4. Add buttermilk to flour mixture; stir quickly with a fork just enough to make a soft dough.
5. Knead dough on lightly floured surface 6 to 8 times, forming a ball.
6. Roll dough ½ inch thick. Cut with floured cutter.
7. Bake for 10 to 15 minutes or until golden brown on ungreased cookie sheet. (I like to rub Imperial Spread on my biscuits after they are done.)

HUSH PUPPIES

Ingredients

- 1 ½ cups catfish coating
- ½ cup chicken coating
- 1 teaspoon sugar
- ¾ cup onion, finely chopped
- 1 cup buttermilk
- 1 egg
- 4 cups canola oil

Directions:

1. Combine catfish coating, chicken coating, sugar, onion, buttermilk, and egg in medium bowl.
2. Heat and oil wok until a thermometer reaches a temperature of 300 °F when placed in oil without touching bottom of wok.
3. Use a small ice cream dipper to drop batter into oil.
4. Deep fry batter until golden brown.

MUSTARD POTATO SALAD

Ingredients

- 2 cups Irish potatoes, cubed
- 2 boiled eggs, cut up
- 6 tablespoons light mayonnaise or ¼ cup plus ⅛ cup
- ½ teaspoon whole celery seed
- 1 tablespoon yellow mustard
- ½ teaspoon plain salt
- ½ teaspoon Lawry's Seasoned Salt
- 2 teaspoons diced pimientos
- 2 tablespoons sweet relish
- 1 teaspoon onion powder
- 1 teaspoon restaurant black pepper
- 1 teaspoon distilled white vinegar

Directions:

1. Peel Irish potatoes (cubed). Cook cubed potatoes on high heat for 13 to 15 minutes. Let sit in hot water for 10 to 15 minutes. Pour potatoes and hot water in colander to drain hot water. Pour cold water over potatoes. Drain. Place potatoes in bowl.
2. Add remaining ingredients to potatoes. Stir ingredients. Store covered in refrigerator until ready to eat.

ROASTED POTATOES

Ingredients

- 4 tablespoons Extra Virgin Olive Oil
- 8 cups Idaho potatoes, peeled (cut into approx. ½ to ¾ inch cubes)
- 2 teaspoons onion powder
- 1 teaspoon Lawry's Seasoned Salt
- ½ teaspoon garlic powder
- 2 teaspoon restaurant black pepper

Directions:

1. Add Extra Virgin Olive Oil to 13 x 8 x 2 inch glass baking dish.
2. Spread potatoes over baking dish. Sprinkle onion powder, seasoned salt, garlic powder, and black pepper over potatoes; stir together. Then spread mixture over baking dish.
3. Bake uncovered at 400 °F for 1 hour, 30 minutes, or until golden brown. Stir potato mixture after cooking for 45 minutes.

MASHED POTATOES

Ingredients

- 2 pounds Irish potatoes, peeled and quartered
- ½ to ¾ teaspoon Lawry's Seasoned Salt
- ¼ cup (4 ounces) Imperial Sperad, softened
- 1 teaspoon restaurant black pepper
- 3 to 4 tablespoons almond milk without vanilla

Directions:

1. Place potatoes in medium saucepan in enough water to cover potatoes. Cover saucepan and bring to a boil. Continue to boil for 20 to 25 minutes or until potatoes are tender; drain. Mash with potato masher or beat with an electric mixer on low speed.
2. Add salt, Imperial Spread, and black pepper. Gradually beat in enough almond milk without vanilla to make mixture light and fluffy.

GARLIC MASHED POTATOES

Ingredients

- 6 medium potatoes or 6 to 7 cups of potatoes peeled and cut up in approximately 2 inch cubes
- 10 garlic cloves, whole
- 5 cups water
- 3 tablespoons Imperial Spread, softened
- ½ teaspoon salt
- 1 teaspoon restaurant black pepper
- 1 teaspoon chicken bouillon (dissolve in 1 tablespoon water; microwave for 10 to 12 seconds)

Directions:

1. Place potatoes and garlic in large saucepan. Add water to saucepan and bring to a boil. Reduce heat to medium; cover and cook until tender when touched with fork.
2. Pour all the liquid off potatoes, but reserve ¾ cup. Mash potato mixture. Add Imperial Spread, salt, pepper, reserved liquid, and chicken bouillon mixture to potato mixture. Stir until smooth.

SCALLOPED POTATOES WITH CHEESE

Ingredients

- 2 pounds Irish potatoes (approx. 5 cups)
- 3 tablespoons finely chopped onion
- 3 tablespoons all-purpose flour
- ¾ teaspoon salt
- ⅜ teaspoon restaurant black pepper
- ¼ cup or (4 tablespoons) Imperial Spread
- 2 ½ cups almond milk without vanilla
- ¼ cup provolone cheese, grated
- ¼ cup extra sharp cheddar cheese, grated
- ½ cup Ramano cheese, grated

Directions:

1. Heat oven to 350 °F. Wash and peel potatoes. Cut potatoes into thin slices to measure about 5 cups.
2. Potatoes are to be placed in a 2 quarts casserole. Arrange potatoes in 4 layers.

a.) 1st layer
- Potatoes (spread on bottom of casserole dish)
- 1 tablespoon onion (sprinkle over potatoes)
- 1 tablespoon flour (sprinkle over potatoes)
- ¼ teaspoon salt (sprinkle over potatoes
- ⅛ teaspoon black pepper (sprinkle over potatoes)
- 1 tablespoon Imperial Spread (dot over potatoes)

b.) 2nd layer
- Potatoes
- 1 tablespoon onion
- 1 tablespoon flour
- ¼ teaspoon salt
- ⅛ teaspoon black pepper
- 1 tablespoon Imperial Spread
- ¼ cup provolone cheese
- ¼ cup extra sharp cheddar cheese

c.) 3rd layer
- Potatoes
- 1 tablespoon onion
- 1 tablespoon flour
- ¼ teaspoon salt
- ⅛ teaspoon black pepper
- 1 tablespoon Imperial Spread

d.) 4th layer
- Potatoes
- 1 tablespoon Imperial Spread
- 2 ½ cups almond milk without vanilla

3. Add Romano Cheese

Uncover and bake 30 minutes or until potatoes are tender.
Let stand for 5 to 10 minutes before serving.

SMOTHERED POTATOES WITH BACON

Ingredients

- 2 tablespoons canola oil
- 5 slices bacon, cut into 2 strips (can use turkey bacon)
- 1 ½ cups water
- 8 cups thinly sliced Irish potatoes
- ¼ cup Imperial Spread (cut up)
- 1 cup chopped onion
- 1 teaspoon white pepper
- ¼ teaspoon salt

Directions:

1. Heat canola oil on medium heat in large skillet. Cook bacon until golden brown on each side. Add water to bacon. Cook on medium heat for approximately 5 minutes.

2. Add potatoes to skillet. Place Imperial Spread and onion over potatoes. Sprinkle potatoes with salt and pepper. Cook potatoes over medium heat until tender. Then reduce heat to low and cook for 30 to 35 minutes. (I serve these potatoes with Hillshire Farm Smoked Sausage. You can microwave sausage until done.) (I cut potatoes in half from long length to long length then thinly slice potatoes.)

BLACKED-EYED PEAS

Ingredients

- 6 cups hot water
- 16-ounce bag dried black eyed peas
- Slab ham
- 2 tablespoons of finely chopped onion
- 1 teaspoon Lawry's Seasoned Salt
- 2 teaspoons restaurant black pepper
- 1/4 teaspoon cayenne pepper
- 1 tablespoon Extra Virgin Olive Oil

Directions:

1. Add Extra Virgin Olive Oil to Dutch Oven. Heat oil on medium heat. Brown ham in oil on both sides on medium to low heat. Remove ham. Set it aside.
2. Add hot water, peas, onion, and seasonings to Dutch oven. Cover and bring to a boil.
3. Return ham to Dutch oven. Cover and reduce heat to low.
4. Cook peas for 2 hours or until tender.

CABBAGE

Ingredients

- 2 cabbages (leaves washed)
- Slab of ham
- 4 cups water
- 2 teaspoons Lawry's Seasoned Salt
- 2 teaspoons restaurant black pepper
- 1 tablespoon Extra Virgin Olive Oil

Directions:

1. Add Extra Virgin Olive Oil to Dutch oven. Heat on medium heat. Add ham to Extra Virgin Olive Oil. Cook ham on medium to low heat until browned on both sides. Remove ham and set aside.
2. Add water to Dutch oven. Cover and bring to a boil. Add salt and black pepper to boiling water.
3. Add cabbage to Dutch oven. Bring cabbage back to boil.
4. Reduce heat to medium; return ham to Dutch oven. Cover Dutch oven; cook cabbage until done (stirring occasionally). Cabbage will be yellowish in color when done.

How to Cut Cabbage

1. Place cabbage on cutting board or cutting surface with stem up.
2. Cut cabbage in half. Cut each half into half.
3. Separate cabbage leaves.

COLLARD GREENS

Ingredients

- 4 bags (10 ounces each) collard greens
- 1 tablespoon Extra Virgin Olive Oil
- Slab ham
- 8 cups water
- 1 teaspoon granulated sugar
- 2 teaspoons Lawry's Seasoned Salt
- 1 tablespoon onion powder
- 1 tablespoon garlic powder

Directions:

1. Wash collard greens.
2. Add Extra Virgin Olive Oil to Dutch oven or pot. Heat on medium heat. Add ham to Extra Virgin Olive Oil. Cook on medium to low heat until browned on both sides. Remove ham from pot and set aside.
3. Add water to Dutch oven or pot. Bring water to boil on high heat.
4. Add ham, sugar, salt, onion powder, garlic powder, and greens (2 handfuls at a time) to Dutch oven or pot. Bring back to boil; cover and cook on medium to high heat until done. Stir occasionally while cooking. Greens are done when withered (slightly darker in color).

CHILI PINTO BEANS

Ingredients

- 3 tablespoons Extra Virgin Olive Oil
- 8-ounce Hillshire Farm Smoked Sausage (sliced into small slices)
- 6 cups hot water
- 16-ounce bag dried pinto beans
- 1 cup white onion, chopped
- 8 large garlic cloves (whole)
- 1 green large bell pepper (chopped)
- 14.5 ounce can whole, peeled, plum tomatoes
- 1 teaspoon restaurant black pepper
- 1 ½ teaspoons chili powder
- 1 teaspoon cayenne pepper

Directions:

1. Add Extra Virgin Olive Oil to Dutch oven. Heat oil on medium heat. Brown smoked sausage in oil on each side. Remove smoked sausage. Set it aside.
2. Add hot water, pinto beans, onion, garlic cloves, bell pepper, tomatoes, black pepper, chili powder, and cayenne pepper to Dutch oven. Cover and bring to a boil.
3. Reduce heat to low and cook for 4 hours.
4. Add sausage to pot 30 minutes before end of 4 hours. (Cook until beans are tender.)

PINTO BEANS

Ingredients

- 3 tablespoons Extra Virgin Olive Oil
- 8 ounces Hillshire Farm Smoked Sausage (sliced into small slices)
- 6 cups hot water
- 16 ounce bag dried pinto beans
- 1 cup white onion, chopped
- 8 large garlic cloves (whole)
- 1 teaspoon restaurant black pepper
- 1 teaspoon cayenne pepper

Directions:

1. Add Extra Virgin Ollive Oil to Dutch oven. Heat oil on medium to low heat. Brown smoked sausage in oil on each side. Remove smoked sausage. Set it aside.
2. Add hot water, pinto beans, onion, garlic cloves, black pepper, and cayenne pepper to Dutch oven. Cover and bring to a boil.
3. Reduce heat to low and cook for 3 hours.
4. Add sausage to Dutch oven 30 minutes before end of 3 hours. (Cook until beans are tender.)

VEGETABLE BEEF SOUP

Ingredients

- 1 pound ground beef
- ¾ cup onion, diced
- 4 cups golden Idaho potatoes, diced
- 24 ounce package frozen mixed vegetables (corn, green beans, English peas, Carrots)
- 1 (46 fluid ounce) bottle V8 Original Sodium 100% vegetable juice from concentrate with added ingredients
- 1 ¼ teaspoons salt
- 1 ¼ teaspoons restaurant black pepper
- 1/3 cup Extra Virgin Olive Oil

Directions:

1. Heat oil in large pot over medium heat. Cook ground beef, onion beef, onion, and potatoes in pot covered until beef is no longer pink; stir occasionally.
2. Add mixed vegetables, V8 vegetable juice, salt, and black pepper to pot. Cover and bring to a boil. Boil for 4 to 5 minutes. Reduce heat to low and cook for 1 hour.

DEEP-FRIED ONION RINGS

Ingredients

- 1 cup chicken coating
- 1 cup buttermilk
- 1 egg, lightly beaten
- 5 medium white onions, sliced into approx. 1/3 inch rings
- Canola oil for deep frying (I use 6 to 7 cups)

Directions:

1. In a medium bowl, mix well chicken coating, buttermilk, and egg. Separate onion slices into rings.
2. Heat oil in a wok for 375 °F. Dip onion rings into chicken coating batter. Fry battered onion rings until golden brown, about 5 minutes. Drain on paper towels.

CREAM CHEESECAKE

Ingredients

- Imperial Spread to grease Bundt pan and cale flour to coat Bundt pan
- One 8 ounce package cream cheese
- 3 sticks Imperial Spread or 1 ½ cups
- 2 cups granulated sugar
- 1 teaspoon vanilla
- 6 eggs
- ¼ teaspoon salt
- 3 cups sifted cake flour

Directions:

1. Do not preheat oven.
2. Grease and flour Bundt pan. Set it aside.
3. In large bowl, cream together Imperial Spread and cream cheese with an electric mixer until fluffy or by hand until well-blended. Gradually add sugar, creaming until light and fluffy.
4. Beat in vanilla. Add eggs one at a time, beating 1 minute after each addition and scraping bowl frequently.
5. In a bowl, stir together flour and salt with a wire whisk. Add wet ingredients, beating after each addition.
6. Pour batter into prepared Bundt pan.
7. Bake at 275 °F for 2 ½ hours. Cool in pan for 15 minutes. Cool cake completely on rack.

APPLE PIE

Ingredients

- My double Crust recipe
- 6 cups thinly sliced, peeled cooking apples (Granny Smith Apples)
- 1 cup granulated sugar
- 3 tablespoons cornstarch
- 1 tablespoon Imperial Spread (cut up)
- ½ teaspoon ground cinnamon
- ¼ teaspoon ground nutmeg

Directions:

1. Prepare and roll out pastry for double-crust pie. Line a 9 inch pie plate with half of the pastry.
2. In a large bowl, stir together sugar, cornstarch, cinnamon, and nutmeg. Add apples and gently toss until coated.
3. Transfer apple mixture to pastry-lined pie plate. Place Imperial Spread over top of apple mixture. Trim bottom pastry to edge of pie plate. Cut slits in remaining pastry; place on filling and seal. Crimp edge as desired.
4. To prevent overbrowning, cover the edge of pie with pie shield or foil paper. Bake in a 375 °F oven for 20 to 30 minutes without pie or foil paper (edge of pie should be light brown). Bake 30 to 40 minutes more or until fruit is tender and filling is bubbly.

Cool on wire rack.
Cut apples in quarters (Cut apples in half, then cut halves into half = 4 quarters)
Slice apple at an angle to remove core. Cut each quarter into thin slices.

RED (KIDNEY) BEANS

Ingredients

- 6 cups hot water
- 16 ounce bag dried red beans or dried kidney beans
- 3 tablespoons Extra Virgin Olive Oil
- Slab ham
- 1 cup onion (chopped)
- 8 large garlic cloves (whole)
- 1 teaspoon cayenne pepper
- 1 teaspoon Lawry's Seasoned Salt

Directions:

1. In Dutch oven, brown ham in Extra Virgin Olive Oil on medium to low heat. Set it aside.
2. Add hot water, red beans, onion, garlic cloves, Lawry's Seasoned Salt, and cayenne pepper to Dutch oven. Cover and bring to a boil.
3. Reduce heat to low and cook for 3 hours.
4. Add ham to Dutch oven 30 minutes before end of 3 hours.

RED (KIDNEY) CHILLI BEANS

Ingredients

- 6 cups
- 16 ounce bag dried red beans or dried kidney beans
- 3 tablespoons Extra Virgin Olive Oil
- 1 cup onion (chopped)
- 1 cup green bell pepper (chopped)
- 1 pound ground beef
- 1 can (14.5 ounces) tomatoes (diced)
- 4 ounce can chop green chilis
- 1 can (8 ounces) tomato sauce
- 1 tablespoon and 1 teaspoon chili powder
- 1 teaspoon Lawry's Seasoned Salt
- 1 teaspoon cayenne pepper
- 4 garlic cloves

Directions:

1. In large skillet, brown onion, bell pepper, and ground beef in Extra Virgin Olive Oil on high to medium heat. Add tomatoes, green chilies, tomato sauce, and seasoning to meat mixture. Cook on high to medium heat.
2. Add red beans or kidney beans and hot water to Dutch oven. Cover and bring to a boil.

Add meat mixture to Dutch oven. Cover and bring back to a boil. Reduce heat to low and cook beans for 4 hours or until beans ae tender.

LEMON ICING

Ingredients

- ½ cup Imperial Spread, softened
- 2 tablespoons lemon juice
- 3 cups pure cane powdered sugar
- 1 teaspoon vanilla extract

Directions:

Combine the Imperial Spread, lemon juice, vanilla, and pure cane powdered sugar. Beat until light and fluffy.

LEMON FROSTING

Ingredients

- 4 cups confectioner's sugar
- ½ cup Imperial Spread, softened
- 3 tablespoons fresh lemon juice
- 1 tablespoon grated lemon zest
- 2 tablespoons almond milk without vanilla

Directions:

In a large bowl, beat confectioner's sugar, Imperial Spread, lemon juice, and lemon zest until smooth. Beat in almond milk without vanilla and increase speed and continue to beat until light and fluffy/ (Can frost one inside layer of a cake and top and sides of a cake.) (Refrigerate cake until serving time.)

BANANA PUDDING

Ingredients

- 3 eggs
- ½ cup granulated sugar
- 3 tablespoons cornstarch
- 2 cups almond milk without vanilla
- 2 teaspoons pure vanilla
- Nilla wafers
- Bananas (sliced)

Directions:

1. Preheat oven to 425 °F.
2. Separate yolks from whites.
3. Beat yolks. Add sugar to yolks. Mix well. Add cornstarch to sugar and yolks mixture. Mix well. Add almond milk without vanilla and pure vanilla extract to cornstarch mixture. Mix together.
4. Cook in top double boiler until mixture thickens.
5. Line the bottom of 9 ¾ x 9 ¾ x 2 inches dish with Nilla wafers (rounded side up). Arrange sliced bananas evenly over Nila wafers. Spread with pudding mixture. Place Nilla wafers on top pf pudding mixture (rounded side up). Place Nilla wafers around the side of dish (rounded side toward outside of dish). Place sliced bananas on top of Nilla wafers. Spread with pudding mixture. Spread with Nilla wafers.
6. Add sugar to egg white; beat until stiff peaks form and sugar dissolves. Immediately spread meringue over banana pudding, sealing to edge of pudding. Bake in preheated oven until meringue is golden brown.

MERINGUE

Ingredients

- 3 eggs whites
- 1 tablespoon granulated sugar

Directions:

1. Preheat oven to 425 °F.
2. In a large mixing bowl, combine egg whites and sugar until stiff peaks form and sugar dissolves.
3. Immediately spread meringue over banana pudding, sealing to edge of pudding.
4. Bake in preheated oven until browned.

CARROT CAKE WITH CREAM CHEESE FROSTING

Ingredients

- 2 cups granulated sugar
- 1 cup Imperial Spread, softened and Imperial Spread and flour for greasing and
- coating cake pan.
- 2 teaspoons pure vanilla extract
- 4 eggs, beaten
- 3 cups sifted cake flour
- 2 teaspoons baking powder
- 2 teaspoons baking soda
- 2 teaspoons ground cinnamon
- ¼ teaspoon ground nutmeg
- 2 cups grated carrots
- 1 ½ cups chopped pecans or walnuts

Directions:

1. Preheat oven to 350 °F.
2. Grease and flour 10 inches Bundt pan.
3. In large mixing bowl, combine sugar, Imperial Spread, vanilla extract, and eggs; beat well.
4. Stir together cake flour, baking powder, baking soda, ground soda, ground cinnamon, and ground nutmeg with a wire whisk.
5. Add grated carrots and chopped pecans or walnuts, stirring until well-blended.
6. Pour into Bundt pan.
7. Bake for 1 hour or until cake springs back when lightly touched with finger.

CREAM CHEESE FROSTING

Ingredients

- ½ package (4 ounce) cream cheese, room temperature
- ⅛ cup Imperial Spread, softened
- 1 teaspoon almond milk with vanilla
- 2 cups powdered sugar

Directions:

1. In medium bowl, beat cream cheese, Imperial Spread, and almond milk with vanilla with electric mixer on low speed until smooth or beat by hand until well-blended.
2. Gradually beat in powdered sugar, 1 cup at a time, on low speed until smooth and spreadable or by hand until smooth and spreadable.
3. Frost cake by zigzagging frosting on cake with decorating bag. Store covered in refrigerator.

LEMON PIE (COOKED FILLING)

Ingredients

- Single Crust recipe (9 inches pie)
- ½ cup cornstarch
- 1 ½ cup sugar
- ¼ teaspoon salt
- 2 cups water
- 3 eggs, separated
- 2 tablespoons Imperial Spread, softened
- ½ cup lemon juice
- 2 teaspoons grated lemon rind
- 3 tablespoons granulated sugar

Directions:

1. Preheat oven to 425 °F.
2. Prepare crust using my Single Crust recipe. Roll out pastry; line pan. Set it aside.
3. Mix cornstarch; sugar, and salt in top pf double boiler. Add water, stirring.
4. Cook cornstarch mixture over hot water until clear, stirring.
5. Bake pastry in preheated oven for 12 to 15 minutes.
6. Change oven temperature to 350 °F.
7. Beat yolks until thick.
8. Pour cornstarch mixture slowly into yolks, stirring.
9. Return yolk mixture to top of double boiler. Cover and cook over hot water until thickened, stirring two or three times. Continue to cook for 3 minutes, stirring.
10. Blend Imperial Spread, lemon juice, and rind into yolk mixture.
11. Pour lemon filling into the crust.
12. Beat whites for meringue. (Use meringue recipe direction). Spread meringue on pie; bake in preheated oven for 12 minutes or until golden brown.

MERINGUE

Ingredients

- 2 to 3 egg whites
- 3 to 4 tablespoons granulated sugar

Directions:

1. Beat whites until foamy. Add sugar, 1 tablespoon at a time; beat until blended after each. Continue beating until meringue forms soft-rounded peaks.
2. Spread meringue on pie, extending slightly onto crust. Bake at 350 °F for 12 minutes.

CHOCOLATE FROSTING

Ingredients

- 6 tablespoons Imperial Spread, softened
- 2 2/3 cups pure cane powdered white sugar
- ½ cup cocoa
- 1/3 cup almond milk without vanilla
- 1 ½ teaspoon pure vanilla extract

Directions:

1. Place Imperial Spread in bowl and beat until creamy.
2. Add sugar and cocoa, mixing well.
3. Gradually stir in milk
4. Stir in vanilla.
5. Spread on cooled cake.

PECAN PIE

Ingredients

- ½ cup golden brown sugar, packed
- 2 tablespoons corn starch
- 1 ¼ cups light corn syrup
- 3 tablespoons Imperial Spread
- ¼ teaspoon salt
- 3 eggs
- 2 teaspoon pure vanilla extract
- 1 unbaked 9 inches pie shell (my Single Crust)
- 1 cup large pieces pecans

Directions:

1. Preheat oven to 375 °F.
2. Mix brown sugar and cornstarch in saucepan. Add corn syrup, Imperial Spread, and salt; warm over low heat just until Imperial Spread is melted/
3. Beat eggs with vanilla. Stir in sugar mixture.
4. Pour into pie shell; sprinkle with pecans.
5. Bake in lower rack of oven at 375 °F for 40 to 45 minutes until filling is set in center. Cool before cutting. Makes one 9 inches pie.

WALNUT PIE

Ingredients

- ½ cup golden brown sugar, packed
- 2 tablespoons corn starch
- 1 ¼ cups light corn syrup
- 3 tablespoons Imperial Syrup
- ¼ teaspoon salt
- 3 eggs
- 2 teaspoon pure vanilla extract
- 1 unbaked 9 inches pie shell (my Single Crust)
- 1 cup large pieces Diamond walnuts

Directions:

1. Preheat oven to 375 °F.
2. Mix brown sugar and cornstarch in saucepan. Add corn syrup, Imperial Spread, and salt; warm over low heat just until Imperial Spread is melted.
3. Beat eggs with vanilla. Stir in sugar mixture.
4. Pour into pie shell; sprinkle with walnuts.
5. Bake in lower rack of oven at 375 °F for 40 to 45 minutes until filling is set in center. Cool before cutting. Makes one 9 inches pie.

SINGLE CRUST

Ingredients

- 1 ¼ cups sifted all-purpose flour, plus extra for rolling
- ⅛ teaspoon salt
- ½ cup Imperial Spread, slightly softened

Ingredients

- 1 ¼ cups sifted all-purpose flour, plus extra for rolling
- ⅛ teaspoon salt
- ½ cup Imperial Spread, slightly softened

DOUBLE CRUST

Ingredients

- 2 ½ cups sifted all-purpose flour, plus extra for rolling
- ¼ teaspoon salt
- 1 cup Imperial spread, slightly softened

Directions:

1. Use a mixture to combine flour, salt, and Imperial Spread in large bowl until well-blended or mix by hand until well-blended.
2. Divide dough in half; shape each half into ball.
3. Roll out 1 ball of dough on lightly floured surface into 12 inches circle. Place dough into a 9 inches pie plate and trim even with edges. Refrigerate until ready to add filling.
4. Wrap the other ball in plastic food wrap; refrigerate until filling is placed in bottom crust.
5. Place filling in bottom crust. Roll out the other ball of dough on lightly floured surface into 12 inches circle. Place rolled dough on top of filling and press dough edges together and crimp edge. Place flour slits in top crust to allow steam to vent.

RED VELVET CAKE WITH CREAM CHEESE FROSTING

Ingredients

- 2 ½ cups sifted cake flour
- ½ teaspoon salt
- 2 teaspoons unsweetened cocoa powder
- ½ cup Imperial Spread, softened and Imperial Spread and flour for greasing and
- coating cake pans
- 1 ½ cups granulated sugar
- 2 large eggs
- 1 ounce bottle red food coloring
- 1 teaspoon pure vanilla extract
- 1 cup buttermilk
- 1 tablespoon white vinegar
- 1 teaspoon baking soda

Directions:

1. Preheat oven to 350 °F.
2. Grease and flour two 9 inches cake pans.
3. Stir together cake flour, salt, and cocoa powder in a medium bowl with a wire whisk. Set it aside.
4. Beat Imperial Spread on medium speed with an electric mixer until fluffy or beat by hand until well-blended. Add eggs, 1 at a time, beating until well-blended after each tradition. Gradually add sugar, beating well. Stir in food coloring and vanilla, blending well.
5. Combine buttermilk, vinegar, and soda in a 16 ounces liquid measuring cup or small stainless-steel bowl. (Mixture will bubble). Add mixed dry ingredients to Imperial Spread mixture, alternating with buttermilk mixture, beginning and ending with flour mixture. Beat at low speed or by hand until well-blended.
6. Pour batter into prepared pans. Bake in preheated oven about 30 to 40 minutes or until toothpick inserted near center comes out clean. Cool cake layers completely on wire rack.

CREAM CHEESE FROSTING

Ingredients

- 1 package (8 ounce) cream cheese, room temperature
- ¼ cup Imperial Spread, softened
- 2 teaspoons almond milk with vanilla
- 4 cups powdered sugar

Directions:

1. In medium bowl, beat together cream cheese, Imperial Spread, and almond milk with vanilla with an electric mixer on low speed until smooth or beat by hand until well-blended.
2. Gradually beat in powdered sugar, 1 cup at a time, on low speed until smooth and spreadable or by hand until smooth and spreadable.
3. Frost cake. Store covered in refrigerator.

PECAN SQUARES

Ingredients

- ½ cup sifted all-purpose flour
- ¼ teaspoon baking soda
- ¼ teaspoon salt
- ½ cup Imperial Spread
- 1 cup brown sugar, packed
- 1 teaspoon pure vanilla extract
- 1 egg, beaten
- 1 cup pecans, broken

Directions:

1. Preheat oven to 350 °F.
2. Grease 8 inches square cake pan with Imperial Spread and flour with all-purpose flour.
3. Stir together flour, baking soda, and salt with a wire whisk.
4. Cream Imperial Spread and sugar together. Add vanilla and egg to Imperial Spread mixture. Stir until well-blended.
5. Add flour mixture to Imperial Spread mixture. Mix well.
6. Stir pecans into flour mixture.
7. Pour batter into 8 inches square cake pan.
8. Bake for 35 to 40 minutes. Cool completely. Cut into blocks. Remove pecan squares from pan.

WALNUT BROWNIES

Ingredients

- ½ cup Imperial Spread
- 2 ounces unsweetened baking chocolate bar
- 1 cup granulated sugar
- 2 eggs
- 1 teaspoon pure vanilla extract
- ½ cup sifted all-purpose flour
- ¼ teaspoon baking soda
- 1 cup walnuts, broken

Directions:

1. Preheat oven to 350 °F.
2. Grease 8 inches square cake pan with Imperial Spread; coat with flour.
3. Stir flour and baking soda together with a wire whisk.
4. Melt chocolate over hot water.
5. Cream Imperial Spread and granulated sugar together. Add vanilla and melted chocolate to Imperial Spread mixture.
6. Add eggs, one at a time, to Imperial Spread mixture.
7. Add flour mixture to Imperial Spread mixture and mix until smooth. Stir walnuts into mixture.
8. Place batter in pan. Bake in preheated oven for 35 to 40 minutes.

BLUEBERRY MUFFINS

Ingredients

- Imperial Spread to grease muffin pan and cake flour to coat muffin pan
- 1 2/3 cups sifted cake flour
- ¼ teaspoon salt
- 2 ¼ teaspoons baking powder
- 1/3 cup Imperial Spread, softened
- ¾ cup granulated sugar
- 1 egg, beaten
- 1/3 cup almond milk with vanilla
- 2/3 cup fresh blueberries

Directions:

1. Preheat oven to 400 °F. Grease muffin pan; coat with flour.
2. Stir together flour, salt, and baking powder with a wire whisk.
3. Combine Imperial Spread, sugar, egg, and almond milk in large bowl. Add flour mixture and mix until smooth. Fold in blueberries.
4. Pour mixture in muffin pan. Bake for 22 to 24 minutes in a preheated oven. Insert toothpick into the center of a muffin to check for doneness. The toothpick will be clean if muffin is done.

YELLOW CAKE

Ingredients

- Imperial Spread to grease cake pans and cake flour to coat cake pans
- 1 cup Imperial Spread, softened
- 2 cups granulated sugar
- 2 eggs, separated
- 2 teaspoons pure vanilla extract
- 2 cups sifted cake flour
- 1 tablespoon baking powder
- ½ teaspoon salt
- 1 cup buttermilk, room temperature

Directions:

1. Preheat oven to 325 °F.
2. Grease and flour two 9 inches cake pans. Set it aside.
3. In large bowl, cream together Imperial Spread and sugar with an electric mixer until fluffy or beat by hand until well-blended. Add egg yolks and vanilla, mixing thoroughly. Set it aside.
4. In separate bowl, stir together flour, baking powder, and salt with wire whisk.
5. Gradually add dry ingredients into wet ingredients, alternating with buttermilk. Mix until fluffy.
6. Beat egg whites until foamy and thick. Fold egg whites gently into batter and mix just until incorporated.
7. Pour batter into prepared pans and spread into even layers. Bake for 35 to 45 minutes or until a toothpick inserted near the center of layers comes out clean. Remove cakes from pans and place on cooling rack. When cakes are completely cooled, frost with desired frosting.

OATMEAL RAISIN COOKIES

Ingredients

- ½ cup Imperial Spread
- ½ cup granulated sugar
- ½ cup packed golden brown sugar
- 1 egg
- 2 teaspoons vanilla extract
- 1 cup sifted all-purpose flour
- ¼ teaspoon baking powder
- ½ teaspoon baking soda
- ½ teaspoon ground cinnamon
- ¼ teaspoon salt
- 2 ½ cups oats
- ¾ cup raisins

Directions:

1. Preheat oven to 375 °F.
2. In large bowl, cream together Imperial Spread, granulated sugar, and brown sugar until smooth. Beat in the egg and vanilla until fluffy.
3. Stir together flour, baking soda, baking powder, cinnamon, and salt with a wire whisk. Gradually beat into mixture. Stir in oats and raisins. Drop a round teaspoonful onto ungreased cookie sheets.
4. Bake 10 to 12 minutes in preheated oven, or until golden brown. Cool slightly. Remove from cookie sheet.

BANANA NUT MUFFINS

Ingredients

- Imperial Spread to grease muffin pans or pan and cake flour to coat muffin pans or pan
- 1 2/3 cups sifted cake flour
- 1 ½ teaspoons baking powder
- 1 teaspoon baking soda
- ¼ teaspoon salt
- 1/3 cup mashed bananas
- ¾ cup granulated sugar
- 1 egg, beaten
- 1/3 cup Imperial Spread, softened
- 2/3 cup walnuts, broken
- ¼ cup almond milk with vanilla

Directions:

1. Preheat oven to 375 °F.
2. Grease muffin pans or pan; coat with flour.
3. Stir together flour, baking powder, baking soda, and salt with a wire whisk.
4. Combine bananas, sugar, egg, Imperial Spread, and almond milk with vanilla in a large bowl. Mix well. Add flour mixture and mix until smooth. Fold in broken walnuts.
5. Pour mixture in muffins pans or pan. Bake for 15 to 20 minutes. Insert toothpick into the center of a muffin to check for doneness. The toothpick will be clean if the muffin is done.

CHOCOLATE CHIP COOKIES

Ingredients

- 1 cup Imperial Spread, softened
- ½ cup granulated sugar
- 1 cup packed brown sugar
- 2 eggs, slightly beaten
- 2 teaspoons vanilla
- 2 ¼ cups sifted all-purpose flour
- 1 teaspoon baking soda
- ½ teaspoon salt
- 1 cup walnuts or pecans, broken
- 1 package (12 ounces) semisweet chocolate chips (2 cups)

Directions:

1. Preheat oven to 375 °F.
2. In large bowl, cream together Imperial Spread, granulated sugar, and brown sugar until smooth. Beat in eggs and vanilla until fluffy.
3. Stir together flour, baking soda, and salt with a wire whisk. Gradually beat into mixture. Stir in nuts and chocolate chips. Drop a rounded teaspoonful about 2 inches apart onto ungreased cookies sheet.
4. Bake 8 to 10 minutes or until golden brown (centers will be soft). Cool slightly. Remove from cookie sheet.

YAM DESSERT

Ingredients

- 29 ounce can of yams
- 1 teaspoon cinnamon
- 3 tablespoons pure cane granulated white sugar
- 3 tablespoons Imperial Spread softened

Directions:

1. Preheat oven to 450 °F.
2. Pour yams juice from can to a container.
3. Add yams to glass casserole dish.
4. Mash yams with potato masher.
5. Add cinnamon, sugar, and Imperial Spread to mashed yams.
6. Pour yams juice into casserole dish with mashed yams. Whisk thoroughly.
7. Bake yams for 1 hour or until golden brown.

BAKED YAMS

Ingredients

- 29 ounce can of yams
- 1 teaspoon cinnamon
- 3 tablespoons pure cane granulated white sugar
- 3 tablespoons Imperial Spread

Directions:

1. Preheat oven to 450 °F.
2. Place yams juice, cinnamon, sugar, and Imperial Spread in uncovered casserole dish. Place in preheated oven without yams. Cook until syrup-like.
3. Add yams and cook uncovered until golden brown (approximately 1 hour).

LEMON ICING

Ingredients

- ½ cup Imperial Spread, softened
- 2 tablespoons lemon juice
- 3 cups pure cane powdered sugar
- 1 teaspoon vanilla extract

Directions:

Combine the Imperial Spread, lemon juice, vanilla, and pure cane powdered sugar. Beat until light and fluffy.

WHITE FROSTING

Ingredients

- ½ cup Imperial Spread, softened
- 3 cups pure cane powdered sugar
- 2 tablespoons almond milk with vanilla

Directions:

1. Beat Imperial Spread with an electric mixer at medium-high speed until creamy.
2. Gradually beat in sugar until smooth. Beat in almond milk with vanilla.

BREAD PUDDING

Ingredients

- 10 slices of bread (cubes)
- ¾ cup sugar
- 3 beaten eggs
- 1 teaspoon cinnamon
- 1 ½ cups almond milk with vanilla
- 1 ½ cups water
- 1 tablespoon Imperial Spread, softened
- 1 cup raisins

Directions:

1. Heat oven to 350 °F.
2. Place bread in an ungreased casserole dish (13 x 9 2 inches)
3. In a large bowl, mix sugar, eggs, cinnamon, almond milk with vanilla, water, and Imperial Spread. Stir in raisins.
4. Pour mixture over bread in casserole dish.
5. Bake uncovered for 55 to 60 minutes.

LEMON BUNDT CAKE

Ingredients

- Imperial Spread to grease Bundt pan and cake flour to coat Bundt pan
- 1 cup Imperial Spread, softened
- 1 ¾ cup granulated sugar
- 4 eggs
- 1 ½ teaspoons lemon extract
- 3 ⅛ cups sifted cake flour
- 2 teaspoons baking powder
- ½ teaspoon salt
- 1 cup almond milk with vanilla
- 1 tablespoon grated lemon peel

Directions:

1. Preheat oven to 350 °F.
2. Grease and flour Bundt pan.
3. In large bowl, cream together Imperial Spread and sugar until fluffy. Add eggs, one at a time, beating after each addition. Beat in lemon extract.
4. In separate bowl, stir together flour, baking powder, and salt with wire whisk; add to creamed mixture alternately with almond milk. Mix until fluffy. Stir in lemon peel.
5. Pour batter into prepared Bundt pan. Bake for 55 minutes to 1 hour or until a toothpick inserted near the center comes out clean. Cool for 20 minutes.

Broiled Parmesan Chicken (see recipe on page 10)

Lemon Pie Cooked Filling (see recipe on page 51)

Deviled Eggs (see recipe on page 27)

Smothered Potatoes with Bacon (see recipe on page 36)

Fried Pork Chops (see recipe on page 21)

Fried Chicken (see recipe on page 12)

Rice Pilaf (see recipe on page 29)

www.ingramcontent.com/pod-product-compliance
Lightning Source LLC
Chambersburg PA
CBRC090827120626
46547CB00008B/620